Fashion Coloring Book For Adults

A Coloring Haven Of Creative Fashion And Beautiful Designs

David LaRocca

2021

INTRODUCTION

Sit back and relax, letting your creativity soar, as you fill in fantastic fashion!

Stuck in a colorless world with your boring 9-5 and stresses of every day life? Then take a moment of tranquility, fill in the pages of the **Fashion Coloring Book For Adults** by David LaRocca and add some colour back into your life!

Release your inner fashion is to and go wild with your pencils within the intricate lines of each unique outfit. Feeling sassy? Cute? How about punkie? Whatever your mood or style, you're sure to find a picture to match.

Delve in and unleash your hidden talent while taking some well-deserved you time!

Let's get right into it…

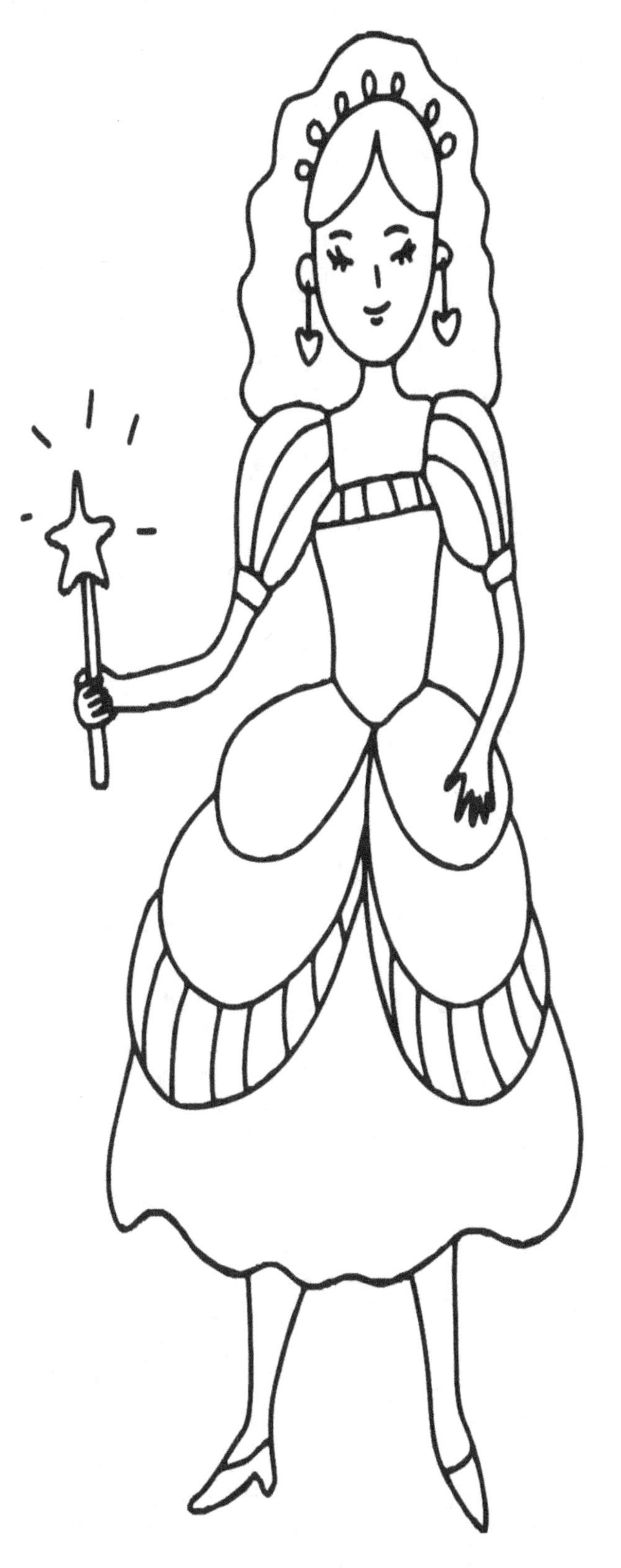

I hope you loved the **Fashion Coloring Book For Adults** as much as I loved creating it ! Follow my Amazon page for more colouring books!

David LaRocca